# EARLY CHILDHOOD IN FOCUS

*Series edited by Martin Woodhead and John Oates*

Early Childhood in Focus is a series of publications produced by the Child and Youth Studies Group at The Open University, United Kingdom, with the support of the Bernard van Leer Foundation.

The series provides accessible and clear reviews of the best and most recent available research, information and analysis on key policy issues, offering clear messages on core policy topics and questions, relevant to the Foundation's three themes of Strengthening the Care Environment, Successful Transitions, and Social Inclusion and Respect for Diversity.

Each publication is developed in consultation with world leaders in research, policy, advocacy and children's rights. Many of these experts have written summaries of key messages from their areas of work especially for the series, and the accuracy of the content has been assured by independent academic assessors, themselves experts in the field of early childhood.

The themes of the series have been chosen to reflect topics of research and knowledge development that address the most significant areas of children's rights, and where a deeper understanding of the issues involved is crucial to the success of policy development programmes and their implementation.

These publications are intended to be of value to advocates for the rights of children and families, to policy makers at all levels, and to anyone working to improve the living conditions, quality of experience and life chances of young children throughout the world.

SERIES EDITORS
Martin Woodhead
John Oates
Child and Youth Studies Group
The Open University
Milton Keynes, United Kingdom

SERIES ADVISERS
Robert Myers, independent consultant, Mexico
Maureen Samms-Vaughan, Executive Chair, Early Childhood Commission, Jamaica

To obtain further copies of this and other publications in the series, visit:
www.bernardvanleer.org

Designed by Agnes Borszeki
Text edited by Margaret Mellor
Printed and bound in the United Kingdom by Thanet Press Ltd, Margate
ISBN 978-0-7492-1274-2

# Early Childhood and Primary Education

*Editors*

**Martin Woodhead**
**Peter Moss**

# EARLY CHILDHOOD IN FOCUS 2

*Transitions in the Lives of Young Children*

## A right to education, without discrimination

The United Nations Committee on the Rights of the Child has provided a General Comment (Number 7), offering guidance to States parties on rights in early childhood under the United Nations Convention on the Rights of the Child, UNCRC (United Nations, 1989), including the right to education.

From General Comment 7:

> The Convention recognizes the right of the child to education, and primary education should be made compulsory and available free to all (art. 28). ... The Committee interprets the right to education during early childhood as beginning at birth and closely linked to young children's right to maximum development (art. 6.2). Linking education to development is elaborated in article 29.1: 'States parties agree that the education of the child shall be directed to ... the development of the child's personality, talents and mental and physical abilities to their fullest potential'. General Comment No. 1 on the aims of education explains that the goal is to 'empower the child by developing his or her skills, learning and other capacities, human dignity, self-esteem and self-confidence' and that this must be achieved in ways that are child-centred, child-friendly and reflect the rights and inherent dignity of the child (para. 2). States parties are reminded that children's right to education includes all children, and that girls should be enabled to participate in education, without discrimination of any kind (art. 2).
>
> *(United Nations Committee on the Rights of the Child, 2005, paragraph 28)*

(See also *A Guide to General Comment 7: Implementing child rights in early childhood* (2006) by the United Nations Committee on the Rights of the Child, UNICEF and the Bernard van Leer Foundation.)

EDITORS

**Peter Moss**, Professor of Early Childhood Provision, Institute of Education, University of London, United Kingdom

**Martin Woodhead**, Professor of Childhood Studies, The Open University, United Kingdom


CONTRIBUTORS

**John Bennett**, Senior Researcher, OECD Starting Strong Intergovernmental Network, Paris, France

**Elizabeth Brooker**, Senior Lecturer, Institute of Education, University of London, United Kingdom

**Sharon L. Kagan**, Professor of Early Childhood and Family Policy, Teachers' College, Columbia University and Child Study Center, Yale University, United States of America

**Thomas Moser**, Professor of Sports Science and Physical Education, Faculty of Education, Vestfold University College, Norway

**Michelle J. Neuman**, Special Advisor on Early Childhood Care and Education, *EFA Global Monitoring Report 2007*, UNESCO, Paris, France

We also acknowledge with thanks the young children's contributions quoted in this publication, and the assistance of those who consulted with children about their perspectives.

ACADEMIC ASSESSORS

**Caroline Arnold** and **Kathy Bartlett**, Co-Directors, Education Programme, Aga Khan Foundation, Geneva, Switzerland

# Contents

# Preface

While considerable progress has been made in achieving education for all, it continues to be the most disadvantaged who are at the highest risk of educational exclusion, underachievement and early drop-out (UNESCO, 2006). Most often, these problems have been conceptualised as about 'children's readiness for school'. Poverty, poor nutrition, and lack of resources and stimulation in the early years have been identified as key factors, leading one group of scholars to estimate that more than 200 million children are failing to fulfil their developmental potential (Grantham-McGregor *et al.*, 2007).

Focusing on children's readiness to benefit from schooling is at best an oversimplification, and in some ways amounts to 'blaming the victim' for the inefficiencies of educational systems. A more balanced view recognises that school systems are currently part of the problem as much as they are a solution to that problem. In resource-poor developing countries that make up two thirds of the world (referred to as the Majority World), the very children who might most benefit from quality education are, as a general rule, least likely to have access to good programmes at either pre-primary or primary levels. These children are also least likely to progress through to school completion, thus perpetuating intergenerational cycles of poverty and inequality (Arnold *et al.*, 2006). The exceptions are encouraging, but they are few and far between. The challenge for policy is, in short, as much about 'schools' readiness for children' as about 'children's readiness for school' (Myers and Landers, 1989).

From a child-focused perspective, this challenge translates into ensuring 'successful transitions'. The rapid growth of early childhood education and care services (ECEC*) means that in many societies these 'transition' issues are becoming more complex, especially where early childhood and primary school policies and services are uncoordinated. Then children may have to adjust to very different environments, expectations and cultures. Of equal concern, the relationship between preschool and school may be coordinated through 'schoolifying' the preschool. Working towards 'a strong and equal partnership' between early childhood and primary provision offers a more positive vision (OECD, 2006a).

Wherever children attend preschools and schools, issues surrounding transition and continuity can appear similar, yet they are played out in profoundly different ways, shaped by political, economic and cultural context, as well as resources, organisation and priorities for early childhood and primary school. Recognising these differences is the starting point for identifying appropriate solutions.

**Martin Woodhead**
**Peter Moss**
Editors

* Many different terms are used to refer to early childhood services for children and families. For simplicity, we refer throughout to 'early childhood education and care', abbreviated to 'ECEC'.

**I.**

# Early childhood and primary education: an overview

*Basic primary education now features in the lives of most of the world's children, and it is recognised as their entitlement.*

*The global challenge is changing, through the rapid growth in early childhood education and care services.*

*Early childhood education and care (ECEC) can make a positive contribution to children's well-being, but services are too often fragmented and uncoordinated with the school system.*

*Increasingly, young children are faced with negotiating a series of pathways, transitions and border crossings during their early childhood.*

# A right to education ... from birth

A major transformation has been taking place in the lives of the world's youngest children, especially in relation to schooling. Where education was once the privilege of a minority, it is now recognised as a universal entitlement, with every child's right to education reaffirmed by the UN Convention on the Rights of the Child, UNCRC (United Nations, 1989). This principle was translated into the *World Declaration on Education for All* (UNESCO, 1990) and in the targets set out in the *Dakar Framework for Action* (UNESCO, 2000). These targets include ensuring that by 2015 all children have access to good-quality primary education, with particular attention to girls, ethnic minorities and children in difficult circumstances. The targets also include expanding and improving comprehensive ECEC, especially for the most vulnerable and disadvantaged children.

Global enrolment in primary education increased from 83 to 86 per cent between 1999 and 2004, with an estimated 682 million children enrolled in 2004. Even so, primary education provision is still marked by inequalities and there are serious shortages in resources available for buildings, teachers and materials. These inequalities are widespread within countries, as well as between countries. As a general rule, the poorest and most vulnerable children and families are least likely to have access to quality education (UNESCO, 2006).

The UNCRC asserts the right of every child to education, without discrimination, and places particular emphasis on making primary education compulsory and available free to all (Article 28). The UN Committee on the Rights of the Child has gone a step further in General Comment 7 (2005), interpreting every child's right to education as beginning at birth and closely tied to the right to development (as set out in Article 6.2 of the UNCRC). The Committee goes beyond a narrow interpretation of 'education' as 'schooling'. Instead, General Comment 7 offers a vision for comprehensive, community services throughout early and middle childhood, both for children and for parents as their educators and caregivers. This vision acknowledges that family and home settings offer the foundation (and for most children the underlying continuity) on which progression through early childhood and primary education is constructed.

**Martin Woodhead**, Professor of Childhood Studies, The Open University, United Kingdom

- *Every child's entitlement to education is now widely recognised, and affirmed by the UN Convention on the Rights of the Child (1989).*

- *Primary education provision is still marked by inequalities in enrolment levels, and serious shortages in resources.*

- *The UN Committee on the Rights of the Child interprets every child's right to education as beginning at birth and closely tied to the right to maximum development.*

*A vision for comprehensive, community services throughout early and middle childhood, for children, and for parents as their educators and caregivers*

# Why go to school?
# Some young children's views

What shall I say? I go to school because I like it. I have lots of friends there. Every day we go to and back from school together. It's good.

*(Girl aged 6, Bangladesh)*

... to learn good habits like not to talk with food in our mouth. We learn to behave well.

*(Boy aged 6, Nigeria)*

I want to be a teacher like my preschool teacher. I want to teach children like her. That's why I want to study.

*(Girl aged 6, Bangladesh)*

My father wants me to be an engineer. If I don't go to school I'll be illiterate. I'll never be able to become an engineer then.

*(Boy aged 6, Bangladesh)*

... so that we can learn and help people. We can become lawyers or doctors and help our parents.

*(Girl aged 6, Nigeria)*

I don't know why children go to schools – it's probably because they have to!

*(Boy aged 6, Fiji)*

Collection coordinated by **Elizabeth Brooker**, Senior Lecturer, Institute of Education, University of London, United Kingdom

# Progress towards universal primary education

The *Education for All (EFA) Global Monitoring Report 2007* confirmed that more and more children (86 per cent) now have access to Grade 1 in primary school. Increases in access between 1999 and 2004 were most marked in sub-Saharan Africa (from 55 to 65 per cent) and South and West Asia (from 77 to 86 per cent). Girls are benefiting from these increases in enrolments. Of the 181 countries for which there are data, about two-thirds have achieved gender parity in primary education enrolments (UNESCO, 2006).

But major challenges remain in the movement to achieve Education for All: 77 million children are still not in either primary or secondary school. Of these, 7 million have dropped out of school, 23 million are likely to enrol late and 47 million are unlikely ever to enrol without additional incentives. India, Nigeria, Pakistan, and Ethiopia account for 22.8 million (two-thirds) of this total (UNESCO, 2006).

While Grade 1 enrolments have risen sharply, too many children who start school do not reach the final primary grade. In the majority of Latin American and Caribbean countries, at least 17 per cent of Grade 1 students do not reach the last grade. This figure was greater than 33 per cent in most of the countries in sub-Saharan Africa. School completion is also low in several South and West Asian countries, including Bangladesh and Nepal. The problems are worst in countries with high poverty, exclusion, and poor-quality schools (UNESCO, 2006).

In general, children are more likely to be out of school if they come from poor households, live in rural areas and have mothers who received no education. In Ethiopia, rural children are 60 times more likely to drop out than urban children. In Burkina Faso, Mali and Mozambique, of the children from the poorest 40 per cent of households, only 10 per cent who entered primary school managed to complete it. In Uganda, Grade 1 enrolments have increased, but half the students that enter school drop out or repeat the first grade. Grade 1 is a revolving door for many children.

**Michelle J. Neuman**, Special Advisor on Early Childhood Care and Education, *EFA Global Monitoring Report 2007*, UNESCO, Paris, France

- *Substantial progress has been made in providing primary education for all children, and greater opportunities for girls, but many children who start school do not reach the final primary grade.*

- *Children living in poverty and in rural areas are least likely to access school, and most likely to drop out.*

*More and more children now have access to school ...
but Grade 1 is a revolving door for too many children*

# Early childhood and primary education

By 2000, most children living in OECD countries (which are among the richest in the world) spent at least two years in early childhood education and care settings before beginning primary school (OECD, 2001). But growth in ECEC is now a global trend. Global estimates suggest that enrolment in pre-primary programmes increased by 11 per cent during the five years up to 2004, by which time 124 million young children were attending some form of ECEC before starting school. Increases were most pronounced in the regions that were also witnessing the strongest growth in primary education, notably sub-Saharan Africa (43.5 per cent), Caribbean (43 per cent) and South and West Asia (40.5 per cent) (UNESCO, 2006).

The provision of services for young children is also marked by inequalities in access and quality. The most disadvantaged children are least likely to have access to quality services, except where innovative programmes specifically target these groups. Institutional organisation and financing, professional training, curriculum goals and pedagogies are all highly variable, especially where provision is decentralised and the private sector plays a significant role, including 'for-profit' and 'not-for-profit' services, which may be unregulated and very variable in quality. The age of transition to compulsory school also varies, as does the extent to which early childhood is separate from or integrated within school systems.

The rapid growth of early childhood services means that increasing numbers of young children and families are faced with the challenge of negotiating multiple transitions during early childhood, for example from crèche – to kindergarten – to Grade 1 – and so on (Myers, 1997; Dunlop and Fabian, 2006). These institutional transitions are very different from the transition from 'home to preschool' or 'home to school'. They involve leaving one setting for another, whereas 'home' is not left behind. For most children, home is their 'secure base', from which they make the daily 'border crossing' to preschool or school, and return at the end of the day. Children's home and community life is a powerful source of continuity. Their parents and older siblings may be active in fostering successful transitions.

**Martin Woodhead**, Professor of Childhood Studies, The Open University, United Kingdom

- *Globally, it is estimated that 124 million young children were enrolled in a pre-primary programme in 2004, an increase of nearly 11 per cent in five years.*

- *The provision of services for young children is marked by inequalities in access and quality.*

- *Increasing numbers of young children and families are now faced with the challenge of negotiating multiple transitions during early childhood.*

*The global education challenge is changing and becoming more complex, through the rapid growth in early childhood care and education*

# POLICY QUESTIONS

- What steps can be taken to realise every child's right to education from birth?

- What policies would overcome the major obstacles to achieving quality education for all, during the early years as well as primary school?

- What can be done to include the children who are most likely to be excluded from early education and primary school?

- How can children's right to quality education be assured in the face of decentralisation and privatisation of ECEC services?

- How has the growth of early childhood programmes altered children's transition experiences, and the role of their parents or other caregivers?

- What policy changes are required at early education and primary school levels to respond to both the new opportunities and the new challenges of ensuring successful transitions?

- How can the views of children (as well as their parents) better be taken into account in addressing these policy issues?

# II

# Successful transitions:
# a question of readiness?

*The concept of 'readiness' has been central in discussions around children's transitions to school.*

*'Readiness' is affected by poverty which undermines parents' capacity to support their children.*

*Family poverty is often linked to school poverty, in terms of accessibility and basic indicators of quality. This raises the question of whether school systems – and individual schools – are ready to support all children at this key transition in their lives.*

*Readiness is best understood as the match between the child and the institutions that serve the child. It requires the participation of families, schools and communities.*

# Readiness – multiple meanings and perspectives

From its earliest use, the word 'readiness' has amassed scores of different meanings, provoked legions of debates, and confused parents and teachers (Kagan, 1990). It appeared in print in the 1920s, with two constructs vying for prominence – readiness for learning and readiness for school. Advanced by developmentalists, readiness for learning was regarded as the level of development at which the individual has the capacity to undertake the learning of specific material – interpreted as the age at which the average group of individuals has acquired the specified capacity (May and Campbell, 1981).

Readiness for school is a more finite construct, embracing specific cognitive and linguistic skills (such as identifying colours, distinguishing a triangle from a square). Irrespective of academic domain, school readiness typically sanctions standards of physical, intellectual and social development sufficient to enable children to fulfil school requirements (Wincenty-Okon and Wilgocka-Okon, 1973).

To complicate matters, a third construct, that of maturational readiness, has evolved. Accepting the school readiness tenet that children should be expected to achieve a fixed standard prior to school entry, maturationists also acknowledge children's individual time clocks. They believe that, because children do not develop at the same pace, they will not achieve the school readiness standard at the same time. Readiness, then, is not determined by chronological age but by developmental capacity (Ilg and Ames, 1965). Quite popular until recently, this perspective has given way to other approaches, especially through the influence of Vygotsky's theories (Vygotsky, 1978). He noted that children grow into the intellectual life around them and that development is actually stimulated by the learning experiences offered in formal settings. Rather than keeping children out of school until they are ready, children need to be in learning environments where adults and peers will nurture their learning and development. This model of 'guided participation' has now been elaborated in relation to early childhood (Rogoff, 1990, 2003) and offers an alternative to readiness concepts.

**Sharon L. Kagan**, Teachers' College, Columbia University, United States of America

- *Readiness concepts have played an important role in debates surrounding transitions.*
- *Readiness concepts have included 'readiness for learning', 'readiness for school' and 'maturational readiness'.*
- *An influential alternative to readiness emphasises how development can be nurtured through guided participation.*

*The concept of 'readiness' has often been used to explain why children fail to make successful transitions to school or drop out altogether*

# Poverty, parents and children's readiness for school

Poverty is one of the most important factors influencing a child's readiness for school. Whether we are talking about families, communities or countries, a lack of resources undermines the capacity to provide adequately for children and to afford them opportunities. Family poverty has been found in a raft of studies to adversely affect children's health, intellectual capabilities, academic achievement and behaviour (Weitzman, 2003). For example, Jamaica's Profiles Project showed the difficulties poor families faced in providing a stimulating environment for their children (Samms-Vaughan *et al.*, 2004). However, we need to avoid over-simplistic conclusions about the relationship between poverty and people's capacity to support children's development. Socioeconomic factors are a key influence, but the picture is more complex.

Where families live in poverty, adults do risk feeling little sense of agency or control, powerless to promote their children's best interests. Too often parents underestimate their ability (through everyday activities and conversations) to support their young children's enthusiasm for learning, their language development and their sense of self. Yet these are the very capacities that have the greatest significance in enabling children to thrive at school and break the cycle of poverty (Arnold, 2004).

In addition, the assumption that programmes focusing on socioeconomic development automatically enhance children's well-being has been overturned. Increased food production does not automatically translate into better-fed children, and better-fed children do not automatically become better-developed children cognitively, linguistically, socially or emotionally. Targeting households does not necessarily benefit the most vulnerable children, unless intra-household priorities are taken into account. While efforts for children should be set firmly within the family and community context, a specific focus on the child is needed, especially in cultures where a child's rights tend to get subsumed under the rights of parents and communities (Arnold *et al.*, 2006).

**Caroline Arnold and Kathy Bartlett**, Co-Directors, Education Programme, Aga Khan Foundation, Geneva, Switzerland

- *Poverty undermines the capacity to provide adequately for children and to afford them opportunities.*

- *Anti-poverty strategies do not automatically enhance children's overall health and development, nor do all children necessarily benefit.*

- *A specific focus on children is needed, especially in cultures where a child's rights tend to get subsumed under the rights of parents and communities.*

*Where families live in poverty, adults feel little sense of agency or control, and it is not surprising that the most disadvantaged families feel powerless to promote their children's best interests*

# Children's readiness for school ... and schools' readiness for children?

The risks that attach to the concept of 'children's readiness' are now widely recognised. Asking about readiness for school places disproportionate emphasis on families' inability to support their children to match the expectations of school. Scholars have increasingly pointed to the flip side of the coin – the readiness of school systems to support children's successful transitions:

> Characteristics that define the 'readiness of schools for children' ... include the school's availability, accessibility, quality, and most important, its responsiveness to local needs and circumstances. These readiness characteristics of schools are influenced by the actions of families and communities as well as by the economic, social, and political conditions of the wider environment.
>
> *(Myers and Landers, 1989, p. 3)*

The consequent challenges facing Grade 1 teachers are often not appreciated:

> In East Africa, a Grade 1 teacher often has 100 children enrolled in her class in the first months of school. The vast majority have not attended preschool before enrolling in primary school. Textbooks – especially in the first weeks or months – may not yet have arrived in the rural schools. The ages of the students range from 4 to 9+ years. The teacher – who is often paid less and treated as lower status than those teaching higher grades – is unlikely to have had specialised teacher training to help her organise, manage and teach the diverse group of students in her class. There may be at most a chalk board and chalk. Some children may not speak the language used for daily instruction. The teacher may well come from another part of the country and may or may not speak the children's home language.

*(adapted from Arnold et al., 2006)*

- *It is important to monitor and improve the readiness of schools for children as well as the readiness of children for school.*

- *School readiness failures are most evident in early-grade classrooms, but the underlying failures are in educational policies, management and resourcing.*

Scholars have increasingly pointed to the flip side of the 'readiness' coin – the readiness of school systems to support children's successful transitions

# Factors affecting schools' readiness for children

Low enrolment rates, poor attendance, grade repetitions, high drop-out rates, and widespread underachievement during the early grades all signal that a school system is not achieving the goal of 'readiness for children'. Factors affecting school readiness include:

- school location, accessibility and admission practices that shape which children are included and which are excluded

- classroom conditions and class sizes, especially overcrowding, which is most common during the early grades

- teacher availability, confidence and commitment, poor teaching methods and harsh discipline, often associated with low levels of professional training and low pay for teachers working with the youngest children

- mismatches between the language and culture of home versus school and more general lack of respect for children's cultural competencies and prior learning

- poor resources and record keeping, resulting in weak learning and inadequate monitoring of student progress.

Too often, these factors combine into self-perpetuating cycles of failure in which early grades become progressively more overcrowded, teachers demoralised, parents and children disinterested and school managers disempowered. School policies, to be truly effective, need to address the whole system in an integrated way (Arnold *et al.*, 2006; Lewin, 2007).

> The 2006 conference of the Association for the Development of Education in Africa (ADEA) in Gabon (ADEA, 2007, online) identified many ways in which schools are not ready for children (especially girls), including long journey times to school, large class sizes, inappropriate curricula, rote-based teaching, shortage of materials, and inadequate teacher training. It also identified ways in which children are not ready for school, due to poverty, poor nutrition, and especially the impact of HIV/AIDS on families' capacities to support their children. The meeting proposed a comprehensive policy framework, addressing organisational and finance structures, inter-sectoral coordination, and partnership approaches to supporting young children in families, communities and school settings.

**Martin Woodhead**, Professor of Childhood Studies, The Open University, United Kingdom

- *If schools are not ready for children, gains made in ECEC programmes may dissipate quickly.*

- *Making schools ready for children requires an integrated approach, addressing the poor conditions for learning and teaching too often found in classrooms.*

*School systems that are not ready for children lead to self-perpetuating cycles of failure*

# Readiness is a condition of families, of schools and of communities

Today, readiness is recognised as a multifaceted construct, referring to the match between the child and the institutions that serve the child (Scott-Little *et al.*, 2006). In other words, readiness is no longer mainly seen as a condition of the child. It is also being seen as a condition of families, of schools, and of communities.

Parenting programmes, family support efforts, and parent involvement activities are all manifestations of this readiness construct. Families are being encouraged to take active roles in the development of children's intellectual life.

Schools carry a major readiness responsibility. Ready schools pay attention to leaders and leadership, school transitions, teacher support, welcoming, supportive and engaging environments, equitable standards and effective curricula, respecting diversity, involving parents, and assessing progress. Guidelines and assessment books to determine schools' readiness have been developed in some US states (Saluja *et al.*, 2000).

Ready schools must exist as part of ready communities, where funding for programmes is adequate, workforce policies are family-friendly, and community commitment to the early years is manifest in public support for a range of health initiatives, social services and family life.

Readiness, while remaining important, is now a prelude to discourse regarding rights – young children's rights to more equitable and excellent services (Woodhead, 2006). As such, 'readiness' may be best regarded not as a fixed construct, but as a theoretical elixir that perpetually evokes new ideas about how young children should best be served.

**Sharon L. Kagan**, Teachers' College, Columbia University, United States of America

- *Children's readiness can be strengthened through supporting parents' engagement with their child's learning and education.*

- *Schools' readiness can be monitored and practical strategies introduced to ensure successful transitions.*

- *Readiness is also a community responsibility, for ensuring that the child's right to more equitable and excellent services is realised.*

*Readiness cannot be only a condition of the child; rather, readiness represents the match between the child and the institutions that serve the child*

# POLICY QUESTIONS

◆ What are the key characteristics of schools that are ready for children, and how can education systems be held to account in this regard?

◆ What steps would be needed to implement specific strategies? For example:

- introduction of health and nutrition programmes within early childhood and primary schools

- provision of special classes and other additional resources and supports for children with language and learning difficulties

- training, recruitment and adequate remuneration of the highest-quality teachers for first grade

- improving classroom resources, reducing class sizes and improving child–teacher ratios

- ensuring curriculum and pedagogy is adapted to the interests, abilities and prior experiences of children, including respect for their age, culture and individuality

◆ How can families be encouraged to engage effectively in their children's education?

◆ What are the most significant obstacles affecting families' ability to support their children to make successful transitions through early childhood and primary education?

◆ To what extent can a sense of ownership of their school by parents and community influence positive early transitions?

◆ How can transitions be monitored during the early school grades, in order to highlight levels of early drop-out and repetition, and draw attention to practices that require reform?

# III

# Early childhood and primary education – a global challenge

*Global growth in ECEC programmes has altered young children's transition experiences, raising new policy concerns and opportunities.*

*One of the arguments for early childhood programmes is that they bridge gaps between home and school, leading to better adjustment to primary school and higher achievement levels.*

*A prominent policy approach has been that early childhood programmes prepare children for the primary grades, which leads to concerns about 'schoolification' of early childhood.*

*An alternative approach envisages a strong and equal partnership, avoiding one tradition dominating the other, and ensuring greater continuity for children.*

# New evidence, new services, new transitions

Global growth in ECEC programmes is in part driven by compelling evidence now available of potential benefits to children and families, including in ensuring that children are more able to adjust to the expectations of school. For many years, the evidence base for policy engagement in the lives of young disadvantaged children relied on evaluations of national programmes initiated since the 1960s, notably HeadStart in the United States of America (Zigler and Styfco, 2004), and especially on small-scale experimental projects, again mainly carried out in the United States (Schweinhart and Weikart, 1980; Campbell and Ramey, 1994). The High/Scope Perry preschool project has been most influential, with startling long-term evidence of children's broader readiness for school, with lower drop-out rates and higher school achievement, lower referral rates to special education, lower dependency on welfare benefits and lower incidence of crime among children selected for a high-quality early education programme compared with a control group. Both experimental and control groups have now been followed up until participants reached the age of 40 (Schweinhart *et al.*, 2004) .

By 1990, positive evidence of the effectiveness of early intervention, including early nutrition and child development programmes, began to be reported from some Majority World studies (Myers, 1992). Nearly two decades later, a review focused on twenty more recent studies meeting six strict criteria, including randomised controlled trial or matched comparison group design. Positive effects were found from parenting and parent–child programmes in Bangladesh, Bolivia, Colombia, Jamaica and Turkey. Evaluations of eight centre-based programmes in equally diverse contexts reported cognitive gains as well as improvements in children's social competencies, and for projects with longitudinal data this was reflected in increases in school attendance, retention and performance. Finally, six comprehensive child development programmes (including the Integrated Child Development Service (ICDS) in India and Proyecto Integral de Desarollo Infantil (PIDI) in Bolivia) demonstrated the benefits of integrated models that include early nutrition and parent support, as well as direct work with children (Engle *et al.*, 2007).

**Martin Woodhead**, Professor of Childhood Studies, The Open University, United Kingdom

- *Quality services in the early years can help ensure that children make a successful transition into primary school.*
- *For many years, advocates and policy makers relied mainly on evidence from a few experimental US studies.*
- *Positive evidence is now available from diverse contexts, including centre-based and parent programmes.*

*A strong evidence base is now available on the potential of early childhood programmes to improve children's readiness*

# Changing transitions

The expansion of early childhood programmes has changed the nature of the transition. Previously, the transition to school 'problem' was defined for the most part in terms of the movement from home to school. Early childhood development and education programmes are (in some people's minds) supposed to help solve that problem. They are supposed to bridge gaps between home and school, leading to better adjustment to and performance in primary school. We have considerable evidence to show that is often the case. But some early childhood programmes seem to do a better job of facilitating the transition than others. And, perhaps more importantly, the general atmosphere of most early childhood programmes is still very different from that of the school. Early childhood education, in many cases, is more closely aligned with principles of holistic care and development, or with making sure children have an enjoyable learning experience, than it is with preparation for formal learning and school settings.

Ironically, the differences between early education and school may create new difficulties for children as they enter school, even as preschool preparation may resolve others. Although children who have attended preschools are generally more ready to learn, and stronger in their basic social, cognitive, and emotional development, they still must overcome the uncertainty and stress associated with moving into a new and different setting. In some cases, under-trained teachers, who are confronted with a mixed group of children with preschool experience and children without, actually push the children with preschool experience aside, ignoring them until the others have 'caught up.'

This has led educational planners to ask:

> What is the point of offering early childhood programming if the primary schools are unprepared for such children?

This, of course, is the wrong question. A better question would be:

> How can we incorporate children's transitions to school and the schools' readiness to receive all children into our early childhood programming and planning?

*(adapted from Myers, 1997)*

- *Traditionally, questions about transitions were mostly about children making the move from home to school.*

- *Early childhood programmes can ease that transition.*

- *Contrasts between early childhood and school programmes can create new difficulties for children.*

*For many young children, the discontinuities between early education and primary school may create new difficulties, even as preschool preparation may resolve others*

# From preschool to primary: children's perspectives

I felt scared because I did not know my teacher. ... My teacher gave orders to us and we had to move quickly or else. I thought of preschool. I did not want to come back the next day. I asked my mother to take me back to preschool. My mother told me my age is not to be at preschool but at class one in the school. School should change to be something like a preschool. I would like to go to a school that is like a preschool in some ways. Some of us children just go to school because our parents told us to do so.

*(6 year old in Fiji)*

At preschool, you go home at a different time. You get to play instead of work, and you only get one break. Once I got to bounce on a bouncy castle, and me and my friends had a really good time, and it was really good. ... There were these things you could ride on and you could climb up on and you could slide down on, and you could play on. We had a gate that we could come in at, and that was really fun.

*(6 year olds, Irish Republic)*

At school there are benches to sit on. There were no benches at preschool. You felt cold if you sat on the floor for a long time. It's more comfortable sitting on a bench.

At our school there are two Apas [female teachers]. One is a bit like the Apa at preschool. Nice. Pretty. She used to be very kind to us. She never scolded or hit us. Of the two Apas in my present school, one sometimes scolds us but never hits us. The other one isn't at all pretty. ... She hits us whether we learn our lessons or not, sometimes for no reason. The Apa in the preschool never hit us.

Now we have to stay at school longer then we did at preschool. Our school starts at nine in the morning and goes on till half-past twelve. And we have to study at home. The Apas give us lots of homework. When we were in preschool there was no homework. We played all the time. ... It was a lot of fun then.

*(6 year olds in Bangladesh)*

Collection coordinated by **Elizabeth Brooker**, Senior Lecturer, Institute of Education, University of London, United Kingdom

*Children may experience uncertainty and stress when moving into a new and different setting*

# Redefining the relationship between early childhood and schooling

One prominent policy approach has emphasised the role of ECEC in preparing children for the school and its long-established culture. This is expressed in programmes for pre-primary education that prioritise children's adaptation to and performance in school, especially literacy and numeracy. These developments have created pressures on early education programmes and have led some to express concern about the 'schoolification' of ECEC, that is the bringing down into ECEC of the traditional aims and practices of compulsory schooling. These pressures don't only come from the school system. Parents' goals for children vary, but early mastery of school learning is often a high priority (Weikart, 1999).

In a few countries, some policy attention has been given to 'carrying upward into primary school, some of the main pedagogical strengths of early childhood practice, e.g. attention to the well-being of children, active and experiential learning, confidence in children's learning strategies with avoidance of child measurement and ranking' (Bennett, 2006). In Sweden, for example, when preschools were brought into the education system in 1996, the then prime minister Göran Persson talked of ECEC as 'the first step towards realising a lifelong vision of lifelong learning', adding that 'the pre-school should influence at least the early years of compulsory schooling' (Korpi, 2005).

If preschools and schools are to be equal partners in the future, one tradition taking over the other must be avoided. Rather, early childhood and primary education services must work together (and with parents and communities) to create a new and shared view of the child, learning and knowledge, recognising '... the child as a constructor of culture and knowledge ... [who] is also active in the construction – the creation – of itself through interaction with the environment' (Dahlberg and Lenz Taguchi, 1994).

This relationship, in which neither culture takes over the other, envisages coming together in a 'pedagogical meeting place' to create and put into practice a common culture. This can form the basis for 'a strong and equal partnership' (OECD, 2001, 2006) between ECEC and school, ensure greater continuity between children's early educational experiences, and foster successful transitions.

**Peter Moss**, Professor of Early Childhood Provision, Institute of Education, University of London, United Kingdom

- *The policy emphasis on children's readiness for school leads to downward pressure on the early years sector, to prioritise preparation for school learning.*

- *An alternative view encourages upward influence of early childhood practices to first grades of school.*

- *A third view proposes a 'pedagogical meeting place' founded on a 'strong and equal partnership'.*

*Early childhood and primary education services must work together to create a new and shared understanding of the child*

# POLICY QUESTIONS

◆ What policies are needed to foster a shared understanding of the child, learning and knowledge so as to create a strong and equal partnership between ECEC and primary schooling?

◆ How can the 'schoolification' of ECEC programmes be avoided?

◆ How can adequate resources be assured for the critical early years?

◆ How can expectations of ECEC and schools best be negotiated among schools, early childhood provisions, families and communities, including putting in place clear lines of communication?

◆ In constructing successful transitions, what is the contribution of professional leadership, at both early childhood and primary phases?

◆ What would be the implication of seeing schools and ECEC provisions as 'hubs' of child rights, linked to all other parts such as health care, nutrition, birth registration, child protection measures and so forth?

IV.

# Towards strong and equal partnerships

*Relationships between primary education and the early childhood sector are often one-sided, with the school system dominating. Policies are needed that work towards a strong and equal partnership.*

*The UN Committee on the Rights of the Child recommends a rights-based approach to early childhood programmes, including initiatives surrounding transition to primary school.*

*There are widespread organisational differences between early childhood and primary school, and associated differences in culture and philosophy.*

*Discontinuities and lack of coordination are common even within OECD countries with well-established education systems. In countries where universal basic education has yet to be achieved, the challenges are even greater.*

*Five major aspects require attention: curricular, pedagogical, linguistic, professional and home-to-school continuities.*

*Children themselves generally approach transitions as a positive challenge. School systems must be organised to respond to that challenge.*

# A strong and equal partnership

The institutional contribution to successful transition presupposes frequent contacts between early childhood services and the school, in the context of a strong and equal partnership. The reality is, however, that relationships between primary education and the early childhood sector are often one-sided. Schools and early childhood centres do not interact with each other sufficiently, often because ECEC tends to be viewed as the weaker partner. This needs to change, and the educational role of the early childhood sector needs to be recognised.

Indeed, pedagogical thinking in the Nordic countries holds that early childhood pedagogy, with its emphasis on the natural learning strategies of the child, should be respected and reflected in the early classes of the primary school. The creation of a special class for children the year before they begin compulsory school, bringing early childhood pedagogy, with its holistic and investigative approaches to learning, into the school, points to the importance of such institutional arrangements.

Schools in other countries provide continuity in educational processes in a different way, through bringing down the sequential and discipline-based educational processes of the primary school into early education. Certain weaknesses are apparent in this approach. Young children placed in an over-formalised, school-like situation from their early years are denied the experience of an appropriate early childhood pedagogy where they can follow their own learning paths and learn self-regulation at their own pace. Research carried out in France, the United Kingdom and the United States of America suggests that while young children from literate and supportive families may do well in instructional classrooms with 20 or more children present, this is not necessarily the case for children coming from low-income and second-language backgrounds (Barnett and Boocock, 1998; Barnett *et al.*, 2004; National Institute of Child Health and Human Development (NICHD), 2000; Shonkoff and Philips, 2000; Blatchford *et al.*, 2002; Piketty and Valdenaire, 2006). Smaller classes and more individual attention are needed for these children. But such ratios and teacher qualifications are strongly resisted by many governments as being both unnecessary and too expensive.

**John Bennett**, Senior Researcher, OECD Starting Strong Intergovernmental Network, Paris, France

- *Currently, some countries encourage introduction of early childhood pedagogy into the early classes of the primary school. More commonly, the pressure is to introduce school-like teaching into early childhood.*

- *Children placed in a school-like situation from their early years are denied the experience of an appropriate early childhood pedagogy.*

*Schools and early childhood centres do not interact with each other sufficiently, often because ECEC tends to be viewed as the weaker partner*

# Successful transitions within a rights-based approach

From General Comment 7:

> The United Nations Committee on the Rights of the Child calls on States parties to ensure that all young children receive education in the broadest sense ... which acknowledges a key role for parents, wider family and community, as well as the contribution of organized programmes of early childhood education provided by the State, the community or civil society institutions. Research evidence demonstrates the potential for quality education programmes to have a positive impact on young children's successful transition to primary school, their educational progress and their long-term social adjustment. Many countries and regions now provide comprehensive early education starting at 4 years old, which in some countries is integrated with childcare for working parents.
>
> ...
>
> States parties have a key role to play in providing a legislative framework for the provision of quality, adequately resourced services, and for ensuring that standards are tailored to the circumstances of particular groups and individuals and to the developmental priorities of particular age groups, from infancy through to transition into school. They are encouraged to construct high-quality, developmentally appropriate and culturally relevant programmes and to achieve this by working with local communities rather than by imposing a standardized approach to early childhood care and education.
>
> The Committee also recommends that States parties pay greater attention to, and actively support, a rights-based approach to early childhood programmes, including initiatives surrounding transition to primary school that ensure continuity and progression, in order to build children's confidence, communication skills and enthusiasm for learning through their active involvement in, among others, planning activities.

*United Nations Committee on the Rights of the Child, 2005*

(See also *A Guide to General Comment 7: Implementing child rights in early childhood* (2006) by the UN Committee on the Rights of the Child, UNICEF and the Bernard van Leer Foundation.)

*Initiatives that ensure continuity and progression help to build children's confidence, communication skills and enthusiasm for learning*

# The policy context: diversities and discontinuities

The age at which children move from preschool into primary school varies considerably, even within OECD countries. In most countries, the age at which compulsory schooling begins (the compulsory school age, CSA) is 6 years, though in a few cases it is 5 or 7. Moreover, in some countries, parents may choose to start their children at primary school before the CSA, between 4 and 5 in Ireland (CSA 6), Netherlands and the United Kingdom (CSA 5), and at 6 in Denmark and Sweden (CSA 7). Class sizes in primary schools also vary. The average in OECD member states is 21.4 children per class, with 16–21 per class in most countries. But the average is over 24 in Japan, Korea, Turkey and the United Kingdom. Similarly, the length of the school day varies. The OECD average for children aged 7–8 years is 758 hours of 'instruction time' per year, but this ranges from 530 hours in Finland to 981 hours in Australia (OECD, 2006b).

These structural differences are often linked to cultural differences, expressed in different understandings (of purpose, of the child and worker, of learning) and practices. The cumulative effect can be considerable.

> For example, a Danish 6 year old will transfer to school from a kindergarten or age-integrated centre which is the responsibility of the welfare system and staffed mainly by pedagogues qualified at degree level but a separate profession from teachers. The average child:staff ratio in these centres is 7.2:1. The first year at school is in a 'kindergarten class', also with pedagogues whose work is guided by a very brief set of curriculum guidelines. Moving up to the first year of compulsory school at 7, children still attend for only about 20 hours a week, and are likely to spend the rest of their day in free-time services, again with pedagogues. A French child will move at the age of 6 years from one school, the *école maternelle*, to another, the *école elementaire*. The average child:staff ratio is 25.5:1 in an *école maternelle*, from which she moves straight into the *école élémentaire* where children attend for about 35 hours a week. In both types of school, she will be with teachers and subject to a detailed curriculum. Continuity is emphasised by the last year of *école maternelle* and the first two years of *école élémentaire* being considered part of the same 'learning cycle'.

In these OECD countries, policy issues surrounding transitions and continuity have been recognised since the 1970s (OECD, 1977; Woodhead, 1979). The policy challenges in the Majority World involve even greater complexity, inequality and lack of coordination, especially where ECEC is growing in a policy context where universal basic education has yet to be achieved (Arnold *et al.*, 2006).

**Peter Moss**, Professor of Early Childhood Provision, Institute of Education, University of London, United Kingdom

- *Organisation and practices vary considerably between early childhood and primary schools. Structural differences are often linked to cultural differences.*

- *The policy challenges in countries of the Majority World are different and in many cases involve even greater complexity, inequality and lack of coordination.*

*The environment into which children move when they enter primary school is not uniform, involving structural and cultural differences*

# Curriculum continuity

Children often experience sharp differences in the curriculum when they begin primary school. Whereas early childhood curricula tend to be organised by domains of learning (cognitive, physical, social, etc.), primary schools often focus on subjects (for example reading, mathematics, science). Shaeffer (2006, p. 7) summarised the challenge thus:

> To ease the transition do we formalize the informal ... or de-formalize what is usually considered formal? Unfortunately the former seems to be the trend.

Some countries have tried to provide more curricular coherence by developing an integrated curriculum for pre-primary and primary school, organised around the development cycles of the child. This approach is taken in the Pre-Primary to Primary Transitions project in Jamaica and the Transition from Nursery School to Primary School project in Guyana (UNESCO, 2006). Sweden has developed three interlinked curricula based on a common set of goals and values for children's learning from age 1 to age 18 years. One risk of such alignment of early childhood and school curricula is the 'schoolification' of early care and education. A possible benefit is that alignment fosters a synergy of cultures (Neuman, 2005).

**Michelle J. Neuman**, Special Advisor on Early Childhood Care and Education, *EFA Global Monitoring Report 2007*, UNESCO, Paris, France

The Step by Step project establishes linkages between preschool and school through its work in 30 Central Eastern European and Commonwealth of Independent States (CIS) countries. Where possible, transitions are planned so that children stay together with their friends as they move from preschool to primary school. Children from first grade are invited to the preschool to talk about their experiences. Preschool teachers and parents review the primary school curriculum together and discuss the skills children need for first grade. Primary school and preschool teachers are trained in the same pedagogic framework and even use the same seven core modules (individualisation, learning environment, family participation, teaching strategies for meaningful learning, planning and assessment, professional development, social inclusion). The organisation of the Step by Step curriculum is based on age, not grade, since primary school entrance age varies. Non-graded classrooms for the first four years of primary (ages 7 to 10) ensure continuity of teaching and learning.

*(based on Arnold et al., 2006)*

- *Children often experience sharp differences in the curriculum when they enter the primary system.*
- *Some countries have tried to develop an integrated curriculum for pre-primary and primary school, fostering a synergy of cultures.*

*To ease the transition do we formalise the informal ...*
*or de-formalise what is usually considered formal?*
*Unfortunately the former seems to be the trend*

# Differences between preschool and primary: some children's views

Here are the perspectives of some 6 and 7 year olds from Lisbon, Portugal.

| Preschool | Primary |
|---|---|
| At preschool we used to play more ... | In primary we work more. |
| We don't do any work there; it's only playing ... | Here we play in the playground and at the after school activities. |
| At preschool we don't work ... only tapestry! | At school we work: we do worksheets, 'My Discoveries' [a commercial set of worksheets] ... |
| At preschool we used to play in the home corner, with cars, we drew, we played on the carpet ... | We play at hide and catch, macaquinho chinês [traditional game] ... we don't play in the classroom! |
| The preschool is beautiful: I used to play, draw some pictures ... | At primary I work and sometimes we learn letters. |
| There we were always in the playground. | Here is different because we do different things ... in primary we work. |
| At preschool I only played! I didn't learn sums, I never read, didn't do any work ... Just painting! | Here yes. |
| Preschool classrooms are for playing ... | Classrooms here are to work. |
|  | Here at primary I work a lot and I get tired ... we cannot play football. |

*(based on Folque, 2002)*

*Children try to make sense of the discontinuities they face*

# Pedagogical continuity

Supporting pedagogical continuity for children as they move from one educational setting to another requires learning environments that foster positive teacher–child interactions. Smaller classes are necessary. Reducing the numbers of children attending school before they reach the normal age for school entry could greatly help address the problem of overcrowded classrooms in some countries (Arnold *et al.*, 2006). The presence of much older children in early-grade classrooms can also make teaching difficult.

It is important for both early childhood programmes and primary schools to focus on continuity of pedagogy and methods across the early childhood age span – from infancy through to age 8 years – if this continuity is to be based on a 'strong and equal partnership' rather than 'schoolification'. Indeed, many Grade 1 and 2 classrooms could benefit from the learning materials commonly found in early childhood centres, for example as in the Releasing Confidence and Creativity programme in Pakistan. Bodh Shiksha Samiti in India and Escuela Nueva in Colombia involve multi-grade classrooms using active curriculum, methods and lesson plans that respond to differing abilities and interests (UNESCO, 2006).

In some cases, closer linkages between early childhood programmes and schools can build on the strengths of both pedagogical approaches. For example, primary schools can become more child-centred, and early childhood programmes can focus more on fostering the skills children need to succeed in school (OECD, 2001).

Planning for pedagogical continuity goes beyond ensuring institutional and curriculum coordination. Teachers and curriculum developers need to take into account the differences within any group of children, in their family circumstances, prior experiences and abilities (Petriwskyj *et al.*, 2005). Accordingly, teachers need to be supported to understand and work with children as unique individuals, which is especially difficult in many parts of the world where early-grade classes are large.

**Michelle J. Neuman**, Special Advisor on Early Childhood Care and Education, *EFA Global Monitoring Report 2007*, UNESCO, Paris, France

- *Pedagogical continuity requires learning environments that allow for positive teacher–child interactions.*
- *Closer linkages between early childhood programmes and schools can build on the strengths of both pedagogical approaches.*

*It is important for both primary schools and early childhood programmes to focus on continuity of pedagogy and methods across the early childhood age span*

# The experience of Norway

The development of kindergarten within Norwegian society was accompanied by both an implicit and an explicit struggle against the traditions associated with school. Mainly this conflict has been – and still is – based on different perspectives on learning and development, children and childhood and, accordingly, different value systems.

It has been claimed that the kindergarten and the primary school are founded on different philosophies, organisational models and pedagogical practices and the transition from one to another needs special attention (Germeten, 1999; Larsen, 2000). Approaches that try to merge the two traditions by a special first grade in primary school, as in Norway since 1997, have been criticised on the assumption that the powerful school will control the pedagogical processes in the first grade, which is not desirable (Haug, 1995, 2005). Rather, the specific pedagogical approach in kindergarten should be applied to the 6 year olds too.

The 2006 Kindergarten Act offers an understanding of the concept of learning very different from a traditional school-based concept. The law emphasises that:

> ... kindergartens shall nurture children's curiosity, creativity and desire to learn and offer challenges based on the children's interests, knowledge and skills.

This expresses an understanding of learning which is neither focused on achievement goals nor mainly controlled by the curriculum. Children are the primary agent of their own learning processes. Kindergartens:

> ... shall lay a sound foundation for the children's development, lifelong learning and active participation in a democratic society ... [and] shall provide children with opportunities for play, self-expression and meaningful experiences and activities in safe, yet challenging surroundings.

Furthermore, the social and cultural tasks of the kindergarten are underlined when the Act states that:

> ... kindergartens shall impart values and culture, provide room for children's own cultural creativity and help to ensure that all children experience joy and ability to cope in a social and cultural community.

**Thomas Moser**, Professor, Vestfold University College, Norway

- *Policy developments around kindergarten and school in Norway can be seen in part as a struggle between different perspectives on children, childhood and learning.*
- *The 2006 Kindergarten Act offers new perspectives, including seeing children as the primary agents of their own learning processes.*

*Recognising the risk of a powerful school system dominating ECEC can be the first step towards implementing a new concept of early learning*

# Linguistic continuity

Linguistic continuity for children is promoted by instruction in their mother tongue and by bilingual programmes, yet monolingual education in the official or dominant language is the norm around the world. Children who learn in their mother tongue for the first six to eight years perform better in terms of test scores and self-esteem than those who receive instruction exclusively in the official language or make an early transition (before age 6–8) to it (Thomas and Collier, 2002). Once a child can read and write in his or her mother tongue, the skills are transferable to other languages. Evidence from Bolivia, Guinea-Bissau, Mozambique and Niger shows that parents are more likely to communicate with teachers and participate in their children's learning when local languages are used (Benson, 2002). In classroom observations across 12 countries in Africa, researchers found that the use of unfamiliar languages forced primary teachers to use ineffective and teacher-centred methods which undermine students' learning (Alidou et al., 2005).

Mother-tongue instruction is also important for promoting gender equality and social inclusion. Girls in some societies are much less likely than boys to be exposed to the official language, because they spend more time at home and with family members. Girls who are taught in their mother tongue tend to stay in school longer, perform better on achievement tests, and repeat grades less than girls who do not (UNESCO, 2005). Multilingual education also benefits other disadvantaged groups, including children from rural communities (Hovens, 2002). If teachers are not proficient in the languages of the children, multilingual family and community members can be rich resources – both in and out of the classroom (UNESCO, 2006).

While recognising the educational benefits of linguistic continuity, schools are often under pressure to introduce the dominant language, starting in the early grades. Parents are strong supporters of early teaching of the dominant language, if they know their children are otherwise likely to drop out after the first few grades. In many countries, children arrive at school with numerous local languages, are then inducted into a regional or national language, but then have to learn English or another global language if they are to progress to higher grades (Woodhead, 1996).

**Michelle J. Neuman**, Special Advisor on Early Childhood Care and Education, *EFA Global Monitoring Report 2007*, UNESCO, Paris, France

- *Mother-tongue instruction and bilingual programmes promote linguistic continuity for children and may be important for promoting gender equality and social inclusion.*

- *Schools are often under pressure, including from parents, to introduce the dominant language, starting in the early grades.*

*Once a child can read and write in his or her mother tongue, the skills are transferable to other languages*

# Home-to-school continuity

Children's transitions can be eased by sharing information and developing ways to involve parents that take into account their preferences and values, and respect ethnic, cultural, linguistic, religious and other forms of diversity (Docket *et al.*, 2000).

- In the Step by Step programme, parents and preschool teachers review the primary school curriculum together and discuss the child's readiness.

- In Pakistan, parents in poor rural communities become resource people, teaching local songs and stories and demonstrating skills such as construction (UNESCO, 2006).

- In France, the *adultes-relais* or 'resource adults' are community mediators who link schools within low-income neighbourhoods to break down communication barriers (Neuman and Peer, 2002).

The role that children themselves play as a source of continuity has been relatively neglected, yet children's siblings, friends and their wider peer group can be highly significant as sources of shared experience and social support, collectively bridging the familiar and the unfamiliar. This is especially true in situations where children feel solidarity with friends in making transitions. Peers can also be a key source for learning, especially where class sizes are large and teachers are unable to give significant attention to individual children (Corsaro and Molinari, 2005). Children themselves are the most significant agents of continuity as they face challenges and make adjustments, negotiating their identities at home, at preschool, and at school.

**Michelle J. Neuman**, Special Advisor on Early Childhood Care and Education, *EFA Global Monitoring Report 2007*, UNESCO, Paris, France

- *Numerous examples are now available of successful strategies for increasing continuity by involving parents effectively in ways that respect their beliefs and values.*

- *Children's role as a source of continuity has been relatively neglected, especially the support and shared experiences of siblings and peers.*

*Early childhood programmes tend to foster parental involvement, yet this is not always carried through into primary schools*

# Professional continuity

Children benefit when early childhood and primary school teachers work together. When staff members communicate and collaborate well, they are more likely to develop compatible programme philosophies and broaden their understanding of children's trajectory from preschool to school (Neuman, 2005). In the Madrasa early childhood programme throughout East Africa, early-grade primary school teachers communicate with teachers from their feeder preschools (Mwaura, 2005). In Guyana, early childhood and primary school teachers work together in school, home visits and other after-school programmes. Such strategies encourage connections and coherence in teaching styles across two distinct levels (Charles and Williams, 2006).

Joint initial training can help teachers develop a common knowledge base and common practices upon which to build partnerships. In England, France, Ireland and Jamaica, for example, primary school teachers are qualified to work with older preschool children and elementary school students. Sweden has taken a broader approach. All teachers, including those working in compulsory school (with children aged 6–16), preschool (with children aged 1–6) and after-school programmes, follow a common core of courses and then specialise in a particular area of teaching. Joint in-service training can also provide an opportunity for staff members to learn from one another and reflect on their own practice. Achieving comparable status and pay for professionals working in different sectors would be desirable in order to equalise power relationships. Early childhood practitioners have traditionally had lower status and training in many countries, compared with primary school professionals. Long-term harmonisation would be desirable; short term, all who work with children should be respected as equal members of the team, bringing different, but valuable, skills, knowledge and experiences to their work with young children (Neuman, 2005). A key source of professional continuity is when professionals working in each sector make respect for the rights of the child their starting point, though this is not yet common practice.

**Michelle J. Neuman**, Special Advisor on Early Childhood Care and Education, *EFA Global Monitoring Report 2007*, UNESCO, Paris, France

- *Where professionals communicate and collaborate well, they are more likely to develop compatible philosophies and practices.*

- *Joint initial training and comparable status and pay can help teachers develop a common knowledge base and common practices upon which to build partnerships.*

*Practitioners with different status and training should be respected as equal members of the team, valued for the diversity of their contributions*

# Achieving successful transitions

The transition from preschool to school is an important moment for many young children. It can be a stimulus to growth and development, but if too abrupt and handled without care it carries – particularly for children from disadvantaged backgrounds – the risk of regression and failure. Transition to school generally has a highly positive connotation for young children. Young children desire to move forward and the challenge of transition can be deeply motivating for them (OECD, 2001, 2006a). For this reason, educators may be encouraged to use the transitions in children's lives far more positively, with greater insight into their potential, rather than seeing transitions as problematic for every child.

To achieve successful transition for all young children, more research is needed on the organisation, aims and pedagogy of both the preschool and the early classes of primary school. The Nordic model, with a rich concept of pedagogy (bringing together concepts of care, nurturing and education), low child:staff ratios, an unhurried approach to young children's socialisation and learning, and its carrying forward of early childhood pedagogy into the junior classes of the primary school, seems to gives excellent results (Programme for International Student Achievement (PISA) 2004). At the same time, the holistic nature of the young child's learning should not be made an excuse to banish sequential learning or emergent literacy and numeracy from the early childhood centre. Young children have a deep desire to communicate and imitate. Their pleasure in using what Reggio Emilia calls 'the hundred languages of children' (Edwards *et al.*, 1995) needs to be nurtured, and can be channelled towards readiness for school, without undue pressure to achieve a pre-specified level of knowledge or proficiency at a given age (Lpfö, 1998).

**John Bennett**, Senior Researcher, OECD Starting Strong Intergovernmental Network, Paris, France

- *More research is needed on the organisation, aims and pedagogy of both the preschool and the early classes of primary school.*

- *The holistic nature of the young child's learning should not be made an excuse to banish emergent literacy and numeracy from the early childhood centre.*

- *Young children have a deep desire to communicate and imitate, which can be channelled towards readiness for school.*

*Young children's pleasure in using 'the hundred languages of children' needs to be nurtured, and can be channelled towards readiness for school*

# POLICY QUESTIONS

◆ How can policy changes:

- foster continuity between ECEC and primary schooling and thereby help to build a stronger and more equal partnership?

- build curriculum continuity around understanding of children's development, in ways that take full account of cultural and individual differences?

- encourage greater pedagogical continuity, including reducing class sizes in early grades, and encouraging more child-centred teaching methods?

- ensure that the culture and language of instruction are based on educational considerations and implemented in the best interests of children?

- promote meaningful involvement, exchange of information and views between parents, ECEC providers and lower primary schools, particularly with a view to ensuring inclusion of more marginalised children and families?

◆ What are best practices regarding training and support for ECEC and primary Grade 1 teachers, especially in relation to literacy and language development – and how do these work out in different contexts?

◆ How can teacher training, in-service training and school organisation best support professionals working together in the best interests of children?

◆ What strategies can be applied in contexts where overall levels of teachers' formal education may be limited, and where there are large status and pay differentials between sectors?

◆ How can young children's own experiences and perspectives most effectively influence developing partnerships in early childhood and primary education?

# References

Alidou, H., Boly, A., Brock-Utne, B., Diallo, Y.S., Heugh, K. and Wolff, H.E. (2005) 'Optimizing learning and education in Africa – the language factor. A stock-taking research on mother tongue and bilingual education in Sub-Saharan Africa', paper presented at the Conference on Bilingual Education and the Use of Local Languages, Windhoek, 3–5 August, ADEA/UNESCO/GTZ.

Arnold, C. (2004) 'Positioning ECCD in the 21st century', *Coordinators' Notebook*, no. 28, Toronto, The Consultative Group on Early Childhood Care and Development.

Arnold, C., Bartlett, K., Gowani, S. and Merali, R. (2006) 'Is everybody ready? Readiness, transition and continuity: reflections and moving forward', background paper for *EFA Global Monitoring Report 2007*, Paris, UNESCO.

Association for the Development of Education in Africa (ADEA) (2007) [online]. http://www.adeanet.org/ (Accessed 14 June 2007).

Barnett, W.S. and Boocock, S.S. (eds) (1998) *Early Care and Education for Children in Poverty: Promises, programs, and long-term results*, Albany, NY, SUNY Press.

Barnett, W.S, Schulman, K. and Shore, R. (2004) *Class Size: What's the best fit?* New Brunswick, NJ, National Institute for Early Education Research (NIEER) at Rutgers University.

Belfield, C.R. and Nores, M. (2004) 'Lifetime effects: the High/Scope Perry Preschool study through age 40', *Monographs of the High/Scope Educational Research Foundation*, no. 14, Ypsilanti, MI, High/Scope Press.

Bennett, J. (2006) *'Schoolifying' Early Childhood Education and Care: Accompanying pre-school into education*, public lecture at the Institute of Education, University of London, 10 May 2006.

Benson, C.J. (2002) 'Real and potential benefits of bilingual programmes in developing countries', *International Journal of Bilingual Education and Bilingualism*, vol. 5, no. 6, pp. 303–17.

Blatchford, P., Goldstein, H., Martin, C. and Browne, W. (2002) 'A study of class size effects in English school reception year classes', *British Educational Research Journal*, vol. 28, no. 2, pp. 171–87.

Campbell, F.A. and Ramey, C.T. (1994) 'Effects of early intervention on intellectual and academic achievement: a follow-up study of children from low-income families', *Child Development*, vol. 65, pp. 684–98.

Charles, L. and Williams, S. (2006) 'Early childhood care and education in the Caribbean', background paper for *EFA Global Monitoring Report 2007*, Paris, UNESCO.

Corsaro, W.A. and Molinari, L. (2005) *I Compagni. Understanding children's transition from preschool to elementary school*, New York, NY, Teachers' College Press.

Dahlberg, G. and Lenz Taguchi, H. (1994) *Förskola och Skola – Tva skilda traditioner och visionen om en mötesplats (Preschool and School – About two different traditions and a vision of an encounter)*, Stockholm, HLS Förlag.

Docket, S., Perry, B., Howard, P. and Meckley, A. (2000) 'What do early childhood educators and parents think is important about children's transition to school? A comparison between data from the city and the bush', paper presented at the 1999 Australian Association for Research in Education Annual Conference, Melbourne, November 1999, Coldstream, AARE.

Dunlop, A. and Fabian, H. (eds) (2006) *Informing Transitions in the Early Years*, Maidenhead, Open University Press.

Edwards, C., Gandini, L. and Forman, G. (eds) (1995) *The Hundred Languages of Children: The Reggio Emilia approach to early childhood education*, Norward, NJ, Ablex Publishing Corporation.

Engle, P.L., Black, M.M., Behrman, J.R., Cabral de Mello, M., Gertler, P.J., Kapiriri, L. *et al.* (2007) 'Strategies to avoid the loss of developmental potential in more than 200 million children in the developing world', *Lancet*, vol. 369, no. 9557, pp. 229–42.

Folque, M. (2002) 'O Jardim de Infância e o 1º Ciclo: o que dizem os meninos' ('Kindergarten and 1st Grade: what the children say'), paper presented at the III Simpósio do GEDEI – Práticas Educativas: Transições e transversalidades, Évora, GEDEI.

Germeten, S. (1999) 'Nærstudier av fem 1. klasser, skoleåret 1998/99' ('Detailed studies of five first classes in the school year 1998/99'), Part Report 2, evaluation of Reform 97 *På vei mot Ny Grunnskole i Oslo* (*Towards a New Compusory School in Oslo*), no. 82-579-0310-8, Oslo, Oslo University College.

Grantham-McGregor, S., Cheung, Y.B., Cueto, S., Glewwe, P., Richter, L. and Strupp, B. (2007) 'Developmental potential in the first 5 years for children in developing countries', *Lancet*, vol. 369, pp. 60–70.

Haug, P. (1995) 'Om politsik styring av utdanningsreformer' ('On the politics of educational reforms'), in Skram, D. (ed.) *Det Beste fra Barnehage og Skole – En ny småskolepedagogikk* (*The best of kindergarten and school – a new pedagogy for young children*), Oslo, Tano.

Haug, P. (2005) 'Rammeplan på tynt grunnlag' ('Framework curriculum on a shaky basis'), *Bedre Barnehager Skriftserie* (*Better Kindergarten Publication Series*), vol. 1, no. 2, pp. 23–35.

Hovens, M. (2002) 'Bilingual education in West Africa: Does it work?', *International Journal of Bilingual Education and Bilingualism*, vol. 5, no. 5, pp. 249–66.

Ilg, F.L. and Ames, L. (1965) *School Readiness: Behaviour Tests Used at the Gesell Institute*, New York, NY, Harper & Row.

Kagan, S.L. (1990) 'Readiness 2000: rethinking rhetoric and responsibility', *Phi Delta Kappa*, vol. 72, pp. 272–9.

Korpi, B.M. (2005) 'The foundation for lifelong learning', *Children in Europe*, vol. 9, pp. 10–11.

Larsen, A.K. (2000) 'Overgang fra barnehage til skole' ('Transition from kindergarten to school'), in Haugen, R. (ed.) *Barn og Unges Læringsmiljø: Fra enkeltindivid til medlem av et flerkulturelt fellesskap* (*Children and Young People's Learning Environment: From individual to multicultural community*), Kristiansand, Høyskoleforlaget.

Lewin, K. (2007) *Improving Access, Equity and Transitions in Education*, Consortium for Research on Educational Access, Transitions and Equity, Monograph 1, Lewes, University of Sussex; also available online at http://www.create-rpc.org/publications/pathwaystoaccesspapers.shtml (Accessed July 2007).

Lpfö (1998) *Läroplan för Förskolan (National Curriculum for Preschool)*. Stockholm, Utbildningsdepartementet (Ministry of Education and Science).

May, C.R. and Campbell, R. (1981) 'Readiness for learning: assumptions and realities', *Theory to Practice*, vol. 20, no. 2, pp. 130–4.

Mwaura, P. (2005) *Preschool Impact on Children's Readiness, Continuity, and Cognitive Progress at Preschool and Beyond: A case for Madrasa Resource Centre Programme in East Africa*, unpublished report. Geneva, Aga Khan Foundation.

Myers, R.G. (1992) *The Twelve Who Survive*, London, Routledge.

Myers, R.G. (1997) 'Removing roadblocks to success: transitions and linkages between home, preschool and primary school', *Coordinators' Notebook*, no. 21, Toronto, Consultative Group on Early Childhood Care and Development (CGECCD) Secretariat.

Myers, R. and Landers, C. (1989) 'Preparing children for schools and schools for children', discussion paper for CGECCD, Toronto, CGECCD

National Institute of Child Health and Human Development (NICHD) Early Child Care Research Network (2000) 'Characteristics and quality of child care for toddlers and preschoolers', *Applied Developmental Sciences*, vol. 4, pp. 116–35.

Neuman, M.J. (2005) 'Global early care and education: challenges, responses, and lessons', *Phi Delta Kappa*, vol. 87, no. 3, pp. 188–92.

Neuman, M.J. and Peer, S. (2002) *Equal from the Start: Promoting educational opportunity for all pre-school children – learning from the French experience*, New York, NY, French-American Foundation.

OECD (1977) *Early Childhood Care and Education: Objectives and issues*, Paris, OECD Centre for Educational Research and Innovation.

OECD (2001) *Starting Strong: Early childhood education and care*, Paris, OECD.

OECD (2006a) *Starting Strong II: Early childhood education and care*, Paris, OECD.

OECD (2006b) *Education at a Glance: OECD Indicators 2006*. Paris: OECD

Okon, W. and Wilgocka-Okon, B. (1973) *The School Readiness Project*, Paris, UNESCO.

Petriwskyj, A., Thorpe, K. and Tayler, C. (2005) 'Trends in construction of transition to school in three western regions, 1990–2004', *International Journal of Early Years Education*, vol. 13, no. 1, pp. 55–69.

Piketty, T. and Valdenaire, M. (2006) 'L'impact de la taille des classes sur la réussite scolaire dans les écoles, collèges et lycées français: estimations à partir du panel primaire 1997 et du panel secondaire 1995' ('Impact of class size on student success in French schools, high schools and colleges: primary panel 1997 and secondary panel 1995 assessments'), Paris, Ministère de l'Éducation Nationale, de l'Enseignement Supérieur et de la Recherche, Direction de l'Evaluation et de la Prospective.

Programme for International Student Achievement (PISA) (2004) *Learning for Tomorrow's World – First results from PISA 2003*, Paris, OECD.

Rogoff, B. (1990) *Apprenticeship in Thinking: Cognitive development in social context*, New York, NY, Oxford University Press.

Rogoff, B. (2003) *The Cultural Nature Of Child Development*, New York, NY, Oxford University Press.

Saluja, G., Scott-Little, C., Clifford, R.M. (2000) 'Readiness for school: a survey of state policies and definitions', *Early Childhood Research and Practice*, vol. 2, no. 2; also available online at http://ecrp.uiuc.edu/v2n2/saluja.html (Accessed June 2007).

Samms-Vaughn, M., Williams, S. and Brown, J. (2004) *Disciplinary Practices among Jamaican Parents of Six-Year-Olds*, Kingston, Jamaica, University of the West Indies.

Schweinhart, L.J., Montie, J., Xiang, Z., Barnett, W.S., Belfield, C.R. and Nores, M. (2004) 'Lifetime effects: the High/Scope Perry Preschool study through age 40', *Monographs of the High/Scope Educational Research Foundation*, no. 14, Ypsilanti, MI, High/Scope Press.

Schweinhart, L.J. and Weikart, D.P. (1980) *Young Children Grow Up: The effects of the Perry Preschool Program on youths through age 15*, Ypsilanti, MI, High/Scope Press.

Scott-Little, C., Kagan, S.L. and Stebbins Frelow, V. (2006) 'Conceptualization of readiness and the content of early learning standards: the intersection of policy and research?', *Early Childhood Research Quarterly*, vol. 21, no. 2, pp. 153–73.

Shaeffer, S. (2006) 'Formalize the informal or "informalize" the formal: the transition from pre-school to primary', *International Institute for Educational Planning Newsletter*, vol. 24, no. 1, p. 7, Paris, UNESCO, International Institute for Educational Planning (IIEP).

Shonkoff, J. and Phillips, D. (eds) (2000) *From Neurons to Neighborhoods: The science of early child development*, Washington, DC, National Academy Press.

Thomas, W. and Collier, V. (2002) *A National Study of School Effectiveness for Language Minority Students' Long-term Academic Achievement*, Santa Cruz, CA, Center for Research on Education, Diversity and Excellence.

UNESCO (1990) 'Meeting basic learning needs', *World Declaration on Education for All*, adopted by the World Conference on Education for All, Jomtien, March 1990, New York, NY, UNESCO; also available online at http://www.unesco.org/education/efa/ed_for_all/background/jomtien_declaration.shtml (Accessed July 2007).

UNESCO (2000) *Dakar Framework for Action: Education for all – Meeting our collective commitments*, adopted by the World Education Forum, Dakar, Senegal, 26–28 April 2000, available online at http://www.unesco.org/education/efa/ed_for_all/dakfram_eng.shtml (accessed July 2007).

UNESCO (2005) *Advocacy Brief on Mother Tongue-based Teaching and Education for Girls*. Bangkok, UNESCO.

UNESCO (2006) *Strong Foundations: Early childhood Care and Education – 2007 Education for All Global Monitoring Report*, Paris, UNESCO.

United Nations (1989) *Convention on the Rights of the Child*, UN General Assembly Document A/RES/44/2, New York, NY, United Nations.

United Nations Committee on the Rights of the Child (2001) *The Aims of Education*, General Comment No. 1, Geneva, Office of the UN High Commissioner for Human Rights.

United Nations Committee on the Rights of the Child (2005) *Implementing Child Rights in Early Childhood*, General Comment No. 7, Geneva, United Nations; also available online at www.ohchr.org/english/bodies/crc/docs/AdvanceVersions/GeneralComment7Rev1.pdf (Accessed June 2007).

United Nations Committee on the Rights of the Child/UNICEF/Bernard van Leer Foundation (2006) *A Guide to General Comment 7: Implementing child rights in early childhood*, The Hague, Bernard van Leer Foundation.

Vygotsky, L.S. (1978) *Mind in Society: The development of higher psychological processes*, Cambridge, MA, Harvard University Press.

Weikart, D.P. (ed.) (1999) *What Should Young Children Learn? Teacher and parent views in 15 countries*, Ypsilanti, MI, High/Scope Press.

Weitzman, M. (2003) 'Low income and its impact on psychosocial child development', *Encyclopedia on Early Childhood Development*, 2003, pp. 1–8.

Woodhead, M. (1979) *Pre-School Education in Western Europe: Issues, policies and trends*, London, Longman.

Woodhead, M. (1996) 'In search of the rainbow: pathways to quality in large-scale programmes for young disadvantaged children', *Practice and Reflections*, no. 10, The Hague, Bernard van Leer Foundation.

Woodhead, M. (2006) 'Changing perspectives on early childhood: theory, research and policy', background paper for UNESCO EFA Global Monitoring Report 2007, *International Journal of Equity and Innovation in Early Childhood*, vol. 4, no. 2, pp. 5–48.

Zigler, E. and Styfco, S.J. (eds) (2004) *The Headstart Debates*, Baltimore, Brookes.

# Photography

Front cover – Nizamuddin, Delhi, India. School. © Wolfgang Schmidt/Das Fotoarchiv/Still Pictures

Opposite p. 1 – San Isidro, Buenos Aires, Argentina. Girl group in a kindergarten in the suburban city of San Isidro near Buenos Aires. © Achim Pohl/Das Fotoarchiv/Still Pictures

p. 3 – Leipzig, Germany. Ferenc (1.5 years) sitting on his mother's lap, reading a book. © Thomas Roetting/Transit/Still Pictures

p. 5 – Honduras, Christian Children's Fund. Children sitting around a notice board listing the "expressions of boys and girls". The programme stimulates children to participate in their own development. © Ruth Cohen

p. 7 – Mozambique. Students in a classroom. © Ernst Tobisch/Still Pictures

p. 9 – Egypt. Kindergarten/nursery school . © Jorgen Schytte/Still Pictures

p. 11 – South Sudan. School Narus. © Sean Sprague/Still Pictures

p. 12 – Mexico. A teacher with a group of children sitting on the floor, having a lesson in an empty classroom. © Ron Giling/Still Pictures

p. 15 – Iran. A woman caretaker assists young girls to do their homework at Maawin Nursery, an orphanage run by Kerman Welfare Organization. These children are victims of the massive earthquake in Bam that destroyed thousands of houses in and around Bam city and killed over 30,000 people in December 2003. © Shehzad Noorani/Still Pictures

p. 17 – Chamiza, Lara state, Venezuela. Meeting of teachers and parents in the village primary school. © Sean Sprague/Still Pictures

p. 19 – Markounda, Central African Republic. Students together in an overcrowded classroom; a boy is showing his writing board. © Ton Koene/Still Pictures

p. 21 – Brazil, Childhood Messengers project (a child-to-child approach to foster the emotional and physical wellbeing of poor rural children under the age of 6). Children playing, boy sliding on a toy. Courtesy of the project.

p. 23 – La Huerta, Honduras, Christian Children's Fund. Denia with preschool teacher Sandra and other students in the background, in front of their preschool. © Elaine Menotti

p. 25 – Bel Ombre, Mauritius. Heritage Golf & Spa Resort, the kindergarten of the hotel. © 123luftbild/Das Fotoarchiv/Still Pictures

p. 26 – Hamburg, Germany. Daily round of talks at the kindergarten. © Markus Scholz/ Argus/Still Pictures

p. 29 – Myanmar. A teacher assists children with education toys for mental development of young children in a preschool run by a Baptist church in North Khway Ye village in Pyay district. © Shehzad Noorani/Still Pictures

p. 31 – Banda Aceh, Indonesia. Muslim boys being taught to pray at a kindergarten in Banda Aceh which lost many of its children to the tsunami, and has now been rebuilt. The school's director Halimah Anwar Bustam describes the horrors suffered: 'The area the kids came from was completely flattened by the waves. On that fateful Sunday the children were in their homes, or many were already on the beach having fun. So many died that morning. It was devastating. Only now are we getting things back together, and are very grateful to CRS who are helping with the reconstruction of our damaged building. The staff give up a portion of their (already low) salaries to sponsor poor children from the outlying villages to come to our school. The new structure includes offices for staff, a library, prayer room and wheelchair-accessible classroom.' Photograph taken in Banda Aceh, mid-December 2006, two years after the tsunami of 26 December 2004 devasted much of the coastal region. Taken to illustrate reconstruction work and projects of CRS (Catholic Relief Services) of USA who sponsored the photo tour. © Sean Sprague/Still Pictures

p. 33 – Indonesia, East Java. Village mosque school. © Julio Etchart/Still Pictures

p. 35 – South Africa. Children in kindergarten, sponsored by the Khulisa Crime Prevention

Initiative. This project works with children and youths to help prevent them from committing crimes.© Jorgen Schytte/Still Pictures

p. 37 – La Huerta, Honduras, Christian Children's Fund. Boy playing with blocks in a preschool. © Elaine Menotti

p. 38 – Indonesia. Girls school. © Mark Edwards/Still Pictures

p. 41 – Kitwa, Zambia. People training at a teachers' school. © Jorgen Schytte/Still Pictures

p. 43 – La Huerta, Honduras, Christian Children's Fund. Enrique playing with empty soda-cans in a preschool run by the 'Madres Guias'. © Elaine Menotti

p. 45 – Philippines, Luzon, Tuguegarao. A teacher helps a student with work in class. © Jorgen Schytte/Still Pictures

p. 47 – Addis Ababa, Ethiopia. A kindergarden; a so-called preschool is cooperating with the IFSO. The children in their green uniforms are having three to four hours of lessons every day. The preschool is run by the church. © Jorgen Schytte/Still Pictures

p. 49 – Oaxaca, Mexico, CIDES (Centro de Apoyo al Niño de la Calle de Oaxaca). Pupil in a CIDES school, Otomie community settlement. © Sara Hannant

p. 51 – Roque Saenz Pena, Argentina. Indigenous pupil in the Gran Chaco near Roque Saenz Pena. © Achim Pohl/Das Fotoarchiv/Still Pictures

p. 53 – Sor Trondelag, Trondheim, Norway. Children rope walking in a *naturbarnehage* (nature nursery). © N. Benvie/Wildlife/Still Pictures

p. 55 – Haiti. Primary school in Maniche. © Sean Sprague/Still Pictures

p. 57 – Israel, East Jerusalem Dissemination Era. Painting outdoors. Courtesy of the project.

p. 59 – Jork, Germany. Theaterkurs für Kinder – Opa beim Besuch der Enkel im Kindergarten (Theatre course for children with the attendance of a grandfather and the grandchildren in the kindergarten.) © Peter Frischmuth/Argus/Still Pictures

p. 61 – Tokyo, Japan. Kindergarten children on a trip in a huge stroller. © (Freelens Pool) Tack/Still Pictures

p. 63 – Berlin, Germany. Erzieherin betreut Kinder beim Zähneputzen in einer Kita in Mitte (Kindergarten, dental hygiene). © Sauer-Hetzer/images.de/Still Pictures

Back cover – Gangtok, India. Shoudlyahs Pradhar from grade 1 of the St Joseph's school, shows his drawing. The school is one of the most renowned in the city of Gangtok which is located in the federal state of Sikkim, India. © Peter de Ruiter